Guy Slater

EASTERN STAR

OBERON BOOKS
LONDON

WWW.OBERONBOOKS.COM

First published in 2018 by Oberon Books Ltd
521 Caledonian Road, London N7 9RH
Tel: +44 (0.) 20 7607 3637 / Fax: +44 (0.) 20 7607 3629
e-mail: info@oberonbooks.com
www.oberonbooks.com

PB ISBN: 9781786826510
E ISBN: 9781786826503

Cover image: Suzanne Dias

eBook conversion by Lapiz Digital Services, India.

Visit www.oberonbooks.com to read more about all our books and to buy them. You will also find
features, author interviews and news of any author events, and you can sign up for e-newsletters so
that you're always first to hear about our new releases.

10 9 8 7 6 5 4 3 2 1

Characters

CHRIS GUNNESS (early fifties)

JAKE HANSARD (late fifties)

U NAY MIN (sixties)

MAYA TUN AUNG (early twenties)

[In 2013 Christopher Gunness went to Yangon in Myanmar to commemorate the 25th Anniversary of the so-called Students' Revolution of 1988 which he had reported on when a young journalist with the BBC World Service. This play is based on events that took place during that visit.]

Low light up on two men asleep in bed.

One of them, CHRIS, starts to twist and move as though trying to escape something. He mumbles anxiously, then moans in fear. His partner JAKE stirs and looks across at him, concerned. CHRIS starts to flinch and shudder emitting liitle yelps of pain, then sits up convulsively, awake. JAKE reaches for him but CHRIS stands and stumbles away trying to shake off the nightmare.

JAKE also gets up and follows him into what is now a living space. CHRIS is still trembling. JAKE takes him by the shoulders and leads him to a chair.

JAKE: Come on… Come on. *(Settles him into chair.)* There. *(Looks at his watch.)* Coffee?

> *CHRIS nods. JAKE goes to turn it on. Silence.*

JAKE: What was all that about?

CHRIS: What?

JAKE: You. Thrashing and moaning.

> *Pause.*

CHRIS: Sorry… Not sure what…

JAKE: Sounded like you were being, I don't know … beaten, whipped.

> *CHRIS doesn't reply, his arms still wrapped around him. JAKE goes back to the coffee. Then –*

CHRIS: Not me.

JAKE: What?

CHRIS: Somebody. Not me.

JAKE: What?

CHRIS: Being whipped.

JAKE: Who?

CHRIS: Some …Not sure.

JAKE: Not sure?

CHRIS: Old demons.

JAKE: *What* demons Chris? *(No reply.)* Bloody demons…

CHRIS: You don't have demons Jake?

JAKE: I talk about mine. What were you dreaming about?

CHRIS: Evaporated… *(Checks his watch.)* God, it's late…

> *He goes to check emails on laptop on table in front of him. JAKE busies with the coffee.*

JAKE: What's your day?

CHRIS: Um … Conference planning meeting. Folk flying in from all over the Middle East to plot and scheme and make mayhem. You?

JAKE: Same old. Hungry?

CHRIS: No thanks.

JAKE: Possible new client in the morning, a little shoot in the afternoon.

CHRIS: Shoot? What?

JAKE: Some high-faluting pasta dishes for Billy's new diabetes cookbook. *(No reply. CHRIS focussed on his mail.)* I *am* charging him this time.

CHRIS: Bloody hell!

JAKE: What?

CHRIS: Crazy!

JAKE: *(Delivers coffee.)* Speak to me, Chris ...

CHRIS: This is ...Got an email yesterday from somebody in Yangon –

JAKE: Yangon?

CHRIS: Oh God...It was ... oh, years ago. Another life, Jake ...From the Chairman of the Committee for the Silver Jubilee Reunion of the 1988 Students Revolution – something like that. Apparently they would be honoured if I could go to Yangon for it.

JAKE: Why you?

CHRIS: It... oh, ...when I was a journalist. A baby.

JAKE: Why don't I know about this?

CHRIS: Because – It's over. Nobody knows about it here.

JAKE: And?

CHRIS: Oh ... BBC World Service sent me to Yangon – still Rangoon then – to ...check stuff out. God knows why me. The only one available I think. Anyway. I happened to be there when a Revolution broke out. I ... got involved.

JAKE: Now they want you to be part of their Silver Jubilee? That's big stuff. Why the hell have you never told me?

CHRIS: I ... guess I thought I had.

JAKE: For fuck's sake, Chris!

CHRIS: Look ... I almost deleted it without replying. But I bashed out a quick two lines thanking them bla-bla but pointing out I have been persona non grata in Myanmar for the last twenty-five years and that I would be arrested the moment I got off the plane.

JAKE: Persona non grata?

CHRIS: I told you. I got involved. So they barred me.

JAKE: What does "involved" mean?

CHRIS: He's just pinged me back. Things are changing fast he says. They have checked with the Ministry, my name has been taken off the list. They would be honoured if I would come. Most honoured, apparently. Bloody hell!

JAKE: So what are you going to do?

CHRIS: Don't know…

JAKE: You want to?

CHRIS: Could be a trap.

JAKE: A trap?

CHRIS: Still a military dictatorship. Prisons still knee deep in political prisoners.

JAKE: So don't. *(Pause.)* You want to?

CHRIS: Don't know.

JAKE: Your nightmare. The man being whipped. Was that Burma?

CHRIS shrugs.

JAKE: You get an email from Burma – Myanmar – and you have a nightmare? Why? What happened there?

CHRIS: It was an important part of my life, Jake.

JAKE: So why does it give you nightmares?

Pause.

CHRIS: I guess …I have… unfinished business.

NAY MIN, followed by MAYA, enters the other side of the stage. They sit cross legged on the floor to meditate.

JAKE: What does that mean?

CHRIS: There is someone there I should see.

JAKE: Who?

CHRIS: A man.

JAKE: Yes?

CHRIS: Called Nay Min.

JAKE: A lover?

CHRIS; What? No … No.

JAKE: So why do you need to see him?

CHRIS: I just do, Jake.

JAKE: And you can't tell me why?

CHRIS: It's complicated.

JAKE: I see.

CHRIS: Oh… hell… Look – If I do decide to go and I get to
meet him – if he is still alive, I suppose and if Military
Intelligence don't clap me in irons the moment I arrive –
then I will tell you when I get back. The whole thing. OK?

Pause.

JAKE: Then go Chris. You know I don't like secrets between us –

CHRIS: Nor do I Jake – but sometimes –

JAKE: We've been here before, Chris.

CHRIS: What? No, no……This was something I put behind
me. Long before we met.

JAKE: What else are you keeping from me?

CHRIS: Nothing – nothing!

JAKE: Good. Go to Yangon and sort it! Going to shower.

Exits.

Lights focus on Yangon apartment. Distant traffic noise. Bicycle bells.

NAY MIN and MAYA meditating on the floor. She is dressed to go to work, he is in longyi and vest.

MAYA gets up and leaves.

NAY MIN continues to meditate.

MAYA reappears with two bowls and two spoons. She puts one on the table, takes the other and goes to sit. She starts to eat.

CHRIS gets to his feet and follows JAKE out.

NAY MIN opens his eyes and stands.

MAYA: Mohinga, Uncle. On the table.

NAY MIN settles in his chair. He starts to eat. After some mouthfuls –

NAY MIN: Very nice. Thank you.

MAYA: I may be a little late. We are busy.

NAY MIN: The hotel is full?

MAYA: Full, full.

NAY MIN: Too many tourists nowadays.

MAYA: Not for us, Uncle.

NAY MIN: No. Yes, I see that, of course. And what will you do today in your hotel that you don't do every day?

MAYA: You know I will do nothing that I don't do every day. I will sit in the office behind Reception and add up numbers and put them in the right columns.

NAY MIN: Will that be interesting?

MAYA: You know it won't be Uncle.

NAY MIN: So. My intelligent young cousin goes to work every day –

MAYA: Uncle! You know why I do it.

NAY MIN: Do I? Let me think now. Oh yes. Soon, am I right, my Maya will own her own hotel?

MAYA: No Uncle –

MAYA / NAY MIN: – A chain of hotels. From Mergui to Myktina.

A muted chuckle from both of them.

NAY MIN: *(Sighs.)* Money, money, money. Your generation –

MAYA: Uncle please!

NAY MIN: No? Am I right? Money, money? Is that really going to be your life child?

MAYA: *(Sighs.)* What else? Over the wall the generals in their castles. Why not a little for us? Politics, all corrupt …What can I do?

NAY MIN: You can fight. Buddhists too can fight.

MAYA; I am not U Nay Min. I am not like you, Uncle. I have to make a life. My life.

NAY MIN: So, so. Yes… It is just… No, no – go to your work, become rich and then you will be able look after me when I am even older and even more feeble. Ignore me, ignore.

She smiles, temporarily reprieved. Gets to her feet.

NAY MIN: Leave the kitchen. Something for the old man to do.

MAYA: The not so old man can write his book.

She makes to leave – then turns back.

MAYA: Uncle – I heard you crying out in the night.

NAY MIN: Yes?

MAYA: You were screaming.

NAY MIN: I was? I am sorry.

MAYA: Were you having bad dreams?

NAY MIN: I disturbed you?

MAYA: As though somebody was beating you.

NAY MIN: I screamed?

MAYA: You sounded frightened.

NAY MIN: Well, well. Only in dreams. I never screamed in life.

MAYA: Why would you, Uncle?

NAY MIN: Oh child… Our worlds so different.

MAYA: Did people beat you?

NAY MIN: *(Sadly.)* Your own story, child, you don't know your own story.

JAKE, now dressed, enters, goes to sit at table with laptop.

MAYA: You don't tell me.

NAY MIN: Would you want to hear? Bad dreams, bad times, bad men. *(Smiles, impish.)* I must have been a very bad man in previous lives to have deserved my present one don't you think?

MAYA: I only know you were a hero. U Nay Min the hero. But –

NAY MIN: Go – you will be late for your work, you will be sacked and then you won't be able to pay for your keep and I will have to look for somebody else and I shall be very sad. Go, go.

He hands her his bowl of mohinga, breakfast finished. She leaves, grateful. He picks up his pad from the table beside him and starts writing as –

Lights refocus to london apartment. CHRIS, dressed, enters with small suitcase.

JAKE: All set?

CHRIS: Think so.

JAKE: Passport?

CHRIS: Check.

JAKE: Tickets?

CHRIS: Check.

JAKE: Visa?

CHRIS: You queued with me!

JAKE: Be happy to drop you.

CHRIS: No, no the taxi is … any minute now. Airport farewells … You know what I am like.

JAKE: Some of the time.

CHRIS: It's only for a few days.

JAKE: Who knows? Do what you have to do.

CHRIS: I am nervous.

JAKE: Of what?

CHRIS: Don't know.

Beat.

JAKE: I rang the Foreign Office.

CHRIS: Did you?

JAKE: They said it was safe now.

CHRIS: Oh Jake… It isn't that.

JAKE: Fine. Well, go and sort it. Whatever. Go and be a star. Christopher Gunness the returning hero.

CHRIS: Yeah, yeah… It was twenty-five years ago.

Beat.

JAKE: And your man, U Nay Min?

Beat.

CHRIS: Yes, of course I will try to see him. I told you. If he's still alive. He must be pushing seventy now…… Oh… to hell with it. Come with me.

JAKE: To the airport?

CHRIS: To Yangon.

JAKE starts to laugh.

JAKE: Oh Chris…

CHRIS: I need you. Come with me.

JAKE: For God's sake…

CHRIS: I am serious. Pack a bag.

JAKE: Visa, visa, visa.

CHRIS: Then tomorrow. Or the day after. Follow me. I am serious.

JAKE: So am I. NO. This is yours. All yours.

Pause. CHRIS checks his watch.

JAKE: Go on, fuck off. I will see you out.

They leave together as –

Lights refocus on Yangon. NAY MIN still writing.

MAYA enters, dressed for work, a shan bag over her shoulder.

MAYA: All right, Uncle?

NAY MIN: Yes, thank you.

MAYA: I will see you this evening

He looks at his watch.

NAY MIN: Ts, ts, ts. You are going to be late for your bus again.

MAYA: Ko Tin Nyo is giving me a lift. He is waiting. Do you want anything?

NAY MIN: What should I want?

MAYA: Don't forget to call my mother.

NAY MIN: I would not dare.

She smiles, turns to go, then stops.

MAYA: No more bad dreams?

NAY MIN: Like a child.

MAYA: Good.

NAY MIN: Ah – no. Before you go – I am sorry but your swain Ko Tin Nyo –

MAYA: He is NOT my swain, Uncle!

NAY MIN: Whatever he is, he will have to wait another few seconds. *(He extricates a newspaper from the pile of papers in front of him.)* Is today the 8ᵗʰ?

MAYA: Yes Uncle.

NAY MIN: Will you do something for me when you finish work tonight?

MAYA; If I can.

He passes across the newspaper open at one of the inside pages.

NAY MIN: Where I have marked. I want you to go.

MAYA: Why?

NAY MIN: I want you to go for me.

MAYA: Why don't you go?

NAY MIN: I was not invited.

MAYA: Nor am I.

NAY MIN: That is different.

MAYA: Why? It says the public is invited.

NAY MIN: I am not the public. I should have been invited. Personally. So, so … I want you to be Nay Min's eyes, his ears

MAYA:I know nothing about Silver Jubilees or 1988 or any of this.

NAY MIN: I think, perhaps, because you don't want to know, child. Now you will learn. Speeches. Always speeches. Very boring. But you will learn. Important.

MAYA: Why?

NAY MIN: Your generation. You only look to the future. You should also look to the past.

MAYA: *(Shrugs.)* Very well.

She turns to leave.

NAY MIN: Not finished … *(She stops.)* There will be a Britisher there. Mister Christopher Gunness. It says – see?

MAYA: So?

NAY MIN: Watch him. Tell me about him, who he talks to, what he says. Watch and tell me everything. But be careful. People will be watching you

MAYA: Why?

NAY MIN: They just will.

Lights refocus to downstage centre. Sound of reception off. Burmese orchestra playing. CHRIS enters with phone.

CHRIS: That's better… Can you hear me?

Light up on JAKE on home phone.

JAKE: Yes. Sorry – is this a bad time?

CHRIS: No, it's fine. Speeches over – I hope – orchestra in full swing. Can you hear? *(Holds the phone away.)*

MAYA moves into to her light, behind CHRIS, watching unobserved.

JAKE: Just about. Gone well?

CHRIS: Sorry?

JAKE: The reunion? Gone well?

CHRIS: Lovely – marvelous. Fantastic. It has been good to see them again.

JAKE: The returning hero.

CHRIS: Utterly undeserved.

JAKE: They sang your praises dutifully?

CHRIS: Lathered me in it.

JAKE: And you cried?

CHRIS: Of course I cried.

JAKE: So all is well.

CHRIS: Yes, Jake.

JAKE: So ... A new dawn?

CHRIS: Sorry?

JAKE: I said – new dawn?

CHRIS: Ah ... Not sure yet. The military are still ... well, the military. But Aung San Suu Kyi we are told is negotiating which is better than being under house arrest. The country still has many problems. How are you? Everything good?

JAKE: Much the same. The flat feels empty.

CHRIS: I will be back in no time.

JAKE: Glad you went?

CHRIS: So far.

Beat.

JAKE: Nay Min? Have you made contact?

Beat.

CHRIS: Not yet. I was hoping to see him tonight.

JAKE: Think he is avoiding you?

CHRIS: Why do you say that?

JAKE: Just what I get from you.

CHRIS: Hope not. The Committee guys went a bit quiet when I asked about him. Maybe there has been a rift. But he is alive at least – and living in Yangon. They say they will try and put me in touch with him.

JAKE: Good.

CHRIS: Jake – you know it's not that.

JAKE: I know, I know. But he is the unfinished business.

CHRIS: Guess so.

CHRIS becomes aware of MAYA.

CHRIS: *(To JAKE.)* Hang on. *(To MAYA.)* Are you looking for me?

MAYA: No, no. I …Sorry.

CHRIS: *(Back to JAKE.)* Look, I'd better show my face back in there. Speak later.

Exits. Light out on JAKE, who also exits.

Refocus on Yangon apartment. MAYA moves to put her shan bag down.

NAY MIN: So, so, so. How was it? A big success? You enjoyed yourself? Tell me, tell me.

MAYA: It was… I don't know if it was a success, Uncle, I don't go to things like that. Many speeches. Food, drink –

NAY MIN: Alcohol?

MAYA: I am afraid so.

NAY MIN: Ts, ts, ts..

They chuckle.

MAYA: I think, yes, I think a success. They were talking about things ... I understood some of it but ... I was only seven months old.

NAY MIN: I know, I know. I well remember you. Wise little eyes even then –

MAYA: Yes, yes ...

NAY MIN: The Lady, was she there?

MAYA: They talked about her. Everybody talked about her. But I didn't see her.

NAY MIN: And him? The Britisher? Mister Christopher Gunness? He was there?

MAYA: He was.

NAY MIN: And?

MAYA: And what? He was ... just there..

NAY MIN: Come on, come on –

MAYA: Everybody seemed pleased to see him. Made speeches about him, too. He made a speech. He cried.

NAY MIN: He cried?

MAYA: *(Giggling.)* Covered his face. Couldn't speak ...

NAY MIN: Why? Did he say why?

MAYA: For the suffering, he said. For our suffering. The suffering of the men in the room. When they were students. And for all who died and were hurt.

NAY MIN: He said that, did he?

MAYA: Yes, Uncle...

MAY MIN: For our suffering...

MAYA: Yes Uncle.

NAY MIN: I see.

MAYA: I have a message for you. From him.

NAY MIN: From Gunness?

MAYA: Yes, Uncle.

NAY MIN: You spoke to him?

MAYA: No. Well ... I didn't really speak to him. It was the Chairman, U Ba Swe, he gave me the message to pass on to you.

NAY MIN: Ba Swe's a fool!

MAYA: How did he know I lodge with you?

NAY MIN: They make it their business to know everything. That is why they are still alive. And what is the message?

MAYA: Mister Gunness says he wants to meet with you. Wherever and whenever you say. *(Silence.)* What would you like me to tell them, Uncle?

Pause.

NAY MIN: You can tell them no. No, no, no, *(Getting to his feet.)* NO, NO NO!!

MAYA is shocked.

NAY MIN: I am sorry ... I ...

He leaves, ashamed.

Lights refocus.Tight spot up on CHRIS on his hotel phone talking to JAKE also in tight spot talking on the home phone.

CHRIS: I have no idea.

JAKE: There must have been something ...

MAYA follows NAY MIN out worried.

CHRIS: Like what?

JAKE: Something from the past, some inkling, some moment when you quarreled, *something*?

CHRIS: No. No. We had a great relationship. We worked well together.

JAKE: He gave no reason?

CHRIS: None that reached me. Just … no.

JAKE: Chris, if you don't tell me what –

CHRIS: There is nothing to tell! I have no idea why he won't see me!

JAKE: And I still have no idea why you want to see him.

Beat.

CHRIS: I know.

Beat.

JAKE: Are you OK?

CHRIS: I am fine. Disappointed, of course. No, I am hacked off! We are here in the same city, we should be talking.

JAKE: So what are you going to do?

CHRIS: I'll ask the Chairman guy, U Ba Swe to try him again. But … I don't know… Ba Swe doesn't like him. I wonder if that is fouling things up.

NAY MIN now in smart aingyi enters comes downstage. He peers into the street below.

JAKE: And if you get no joy?

CHRIS: Well … Yes. Yes I will come home. Of course.

JAKE: And nothing resolved.

CHRIS: I guess not.

Lights down on CHRIS and JAKE who exit.

Refocus on Yangon apartment, NAY MIN at DS "window" still peering down.

MAYA enters.

MAYA: I am going now Uncle.

NAY MIN: *(Looking at his watch.)* Already?

MAYA: Fish for your lunch. Fried nice and crisp the way you like it. And rice in the pot.

NAY MIN: Wait, wait …Where are you going my dear?

MAYA: Not sure. Maybe a walk round Inya Lake, maybe a film.

NAY MIN: So many ways to spend a day off. Good, good. Choices, excellent. By yourself? Be careful now. Some young men… You understand?

MAYA: I understand, Uncle,

NAY MIN: I am *in loco parentis.*

MAYA: I am seeing a friend, that's all.

NAY MIN: And who is that?

MAYA: She's called Kyi Kyi.

NAY MIN: Kyi Kyi? Tell me about Ky Kyi.

MAYA: But Uncle –

NAY MIN: Come – come sit with me. *(He sits, patting the place beside him. Reluctantly she joins him.)* So … Who is this Kyi Kyi?

23

MAYA: A friend. She works for an NGO. Norwegian.

NAY MIN: A Norwegian NGO? Very good. And how did you meet her?

MAYA: Uncle why are you asking all this?

NAY MIN: I told you. I am *in loco parentis.*

MAYA: I know, Uncle.

NAY MIN: So, so ... The fish is fried?

MAYA: Yes, Uncle.

NAY MIN: Nice and crisp? Not too much oil? Plenty of turmeric?

MAYA: Of course.

NAY MIN: Aiyee... What a lucky man I am.

MAYA: *(Exasperated.)* Uncle –

The door bell goes.

MAYA freezes. Visitors are rare – and possibly dangerous. NAY MIN glances at his watch.

NAY MIN: Go, go, answer. Please.

MAYA: Who is it?

NAY MIN: The door. Please.

MAYA: You are expecting someone?

NAY MIN: Go, go. Please.

MAYA: Uncle, why are you dressed up today? Who are you expecting?

The bell goes again. She turns to NAY MIN.

MAYA: It's him, isn't it? You've agreed to meet him. You've changed your mind. Why?

NAY MIN: You must be my witness! Very important. Listen to everything he says. Everything!

MAYA: Why? ... What ...

NAY MIN: You are my witness. Remember. The door. Please.

She exits. We hear door opening.

CHRIS: *(Off.)* Good morning. Is U May Min at home?

NAY MIN: *(Calling.)* Come! Come!

We hear front door shut. CHRIS enters, followed by MAYA.

A moment as the two men regard each other.

CHRIS: Eastern Star...

NAY MIN puts out his hand. CHRIS takes it, then folds him in a big bear hug.

CHRIS: Thank you. Thank you for seeing me.

NAY MIN extricates himself, not tactile.

NAY MIN: Mister Christopher this is Maya. Maya this is the famous Chris Gunness.

CHRIS offers his hand.

CHRIS: Hello Maya ... I saw you at the Reception the other night, didn't I?

NAY MIN: My spy! I sent her as my spy.

CHRIS: Your spy? *(Back to MAYA.)* You followed me!

MAYA: *(Embarrassed. Releasing his hand.)* Uncle ...

NAY MIN: No, no, you have to stay. For a little, for a little. You must know Mister Christopher, learn from him. Part of your history. Very important.

MAYA: But –

NAY MIN: She is meeting her friend. Well, I am afraid friend Ky Kyi will just have to wait. This is important.

MAYA: Not just Ky Kyi, Uncle –

She checks herself.

NAY MIN: Oh! I see! Your swain is downstairs.

MAYA: Uncle, he is NOT my swain and he is just driving me to meet Ky Kyi and –

NAY MIN: I understand. He is waiting. Well go down stairs and tell him he will have to wait a little longer. You will call him. Soon. One hour. Tell him anything. Go, go.

He hustles her out of the flat. Turns back to CHRIS.

NAY MIN: My cousin's daughter. But I think of her as a cousin and she thinks of me as her Uncle. Which I am pleased to be. Her mother lives up in Maymyo. Maya is ambitious, wants to make her career in Yangon. Arrived last month. She lodges in my guest bedroom. And looks after me.

CHRIS: Sounds good to me. But I am sorry if I have caused – -

NAY MIN: No, no. I want her to stay. To listen to you. My plan. That generation, they know nothing of that time. And it is important!

CHRIS: I agree.

NAY MIN: She is pretty, no? Do you think she is pretty?

CHRIS: Well –

NAY MIN: Smart. Smart young woman. Tells me she never wants to get married. That she will never submit to a man. But I am not so sure. Maybe she has secrets. Well we all have secrets, not so? *(Chuckles.)* What advice can I give her? Just an old bachelor. Well ... Look at you! Christopher Gunness. Back in Burma.

CHRIS: You look good. Just the same.

NAY MIN: I do?

CHRIS: Well... a little older perhaps.

NAY MIN: Older – yes. Hah. The scar? You don't see it?

CHRIS: I ...

NAY MIN points to his jaw line.

NAY MIN: Good surgery, no?

CHRIS: Surgery?

NAY MIN: They broke my jaw. In prison.

CHRIS: Oh my God...

NAY MIN: Hit in the mouth. *(Gestures.)* So!.... There was a doctor. Also prisoner. He mended it. Needle and thread! *(Demonstrates, laughing.)* Lucky, no?

CHRIS speechless.

NAY MIN: Jaw, teeth. All broken. Yes...So, so, so. You look well. Put on weight.

CHRIS: Oh... Yes, I am afraid I have.

NAY MIN: What happened? Did you get married?

CHRIS hesitates.

CHRIS: I did as a matter of fact.

NAY MIN: Excellent! Tell me about her.

Beat.

CHRIS: He's a photographer. From Canada.

Beat.

NAY MIN: A man? You married a man?

CHRIS: That's right.

NAY MIN: So, so, so. ... You know when you were here I always thought ... You know...

CHRIS: What?

NAY MIN: That you were like a girl. Girly.

CHRIS: *(Laughing.)* Eastern Star – that's just terrible, you are a human rights lawyer!

NAY MIN: Is it? Terrible? Well... yes, yes. I have read about it. I am just not used –

CHRIS: That's OK.

MAYA re-enters.

NAY MIN: Good, good. Your swain has accepted his fate?

MAYA: He is NOT my – ! Yes uncle...

NAY MIN: Good. I need you here. We need you here. You will learn. Be our witness – no? Already I have learned new things. Mister Christopher has got married. To a man.

As NAY MIN planned she is also nonplussed.

MAYA: Ah...

NAY MIN: Yes ... *(Back to CHRIS.)* And what else has happened to you?

Beat.

CHRIS: Oh ... Well ... I have been very lucky.

NAY MIN: We have google now. I have read about you. International figure United Nations Representative. Big shot.

CHRIS: It sounds more important than –

NAY MIN: And you are rich? Big money? Big house?

CHRIS: Not ... not BIG money. No, yes, I ... I have been very lucky.

NAY MIN: Good... good.

Beat.

CHRIS: I thought you had decided you didn't want to see me.

NAY MIN: I changed my mind.

CHRIS: Why?

NAY MIN: For reasons.

CHRIS: What reasons?

NAY MIN: I decided I needed to know.

CHRIS: Know what?

Beat.

NAY MIN: Why have you been to Myanmar many times and not come to see me?

CHRIS: *What?*

NAY MIN: Why?

CHRIS: Who told you that? That is nonsense!

NAY MIN: Nonsense?

CHRIS: Of course I haven't! And why would I not want to see you?

NAY MIN: That is what I want to know.

CHRIS: What possible reason could there be?

NAY MIN: Because the Generals had paid for you.

CHRIS: I can't believe this. You thought I was on their side? They had bought me?

NAY MIN: Not so?

CHRIS: How could you ... After all that we ... I am so sad – no I am *angry* that you could think that – even for a moment.

NAY MIN: You are telling the truth?

CHRIS: Nay Min – for God's sake –

MAYA: Uncle –

NAY MIN: He is telling the truth? Telling the truth? *(Searching between CHRIS and MAYA.)* Yes. Good. Yes. Very well. Telling the truth. I believe. I am pleased. I am sorry, Mister Christopher. In prison ... so much time to think. Many thoughts grow. Bad thoughts. Don't be angry. That's my job!

NAY MIN smiles, puts his hand out and rests it on CHRIS's arm. Impulsively CHRIS hugs him. After a moment NAY MIN breaks away

NAY MIN: *(As though talking to himself.)* So difficult, so difficult... I must not be angry. Must NOT!...

CHRIS: I...

NAY MIN: No, no. Foolishness, foolishness ... I am good, all
good ... What can I say? I have learned not to trust. You
must understand.

CHRIS: Was that really why you did not want to see me? You
thought I had been bought?

NAY MIN: Perhaps, perhaps. That and ... oh so many things,
so many things, so many difficult things ... Does it matter?
We are talking.

CHRIS: Yes ... Yes ... So ... And you – are you practicing as a
lawyer?

NAY MIN: They took my license away, did you know?

CHRIS: No.

INAY MIN: No matter. I help people sometimes. *(Impish
again, gesturing round the room.)* My chambers. Not entirely
forgotten. After so many years in prison I think that is
good.

CHRIS: It is – it *is* good ... Forgotten. How could you be
forgotten? ... I ... That is one reason I wanted so much to
see you.

NAY MIN: Yes?

Beat.

NAY MIN: So?

CHRIS: I thought... I have often wondered if ... I just wanted
to ask if – *(Suddenly constrained by MAYA's presence.)* I don't
know whether –

NAY MIN: No, no. My Maya must know everything. She
asked me to tell her. My story. Our story. Now you will tell
her. You are here, the man who has come back. We will
tell her together.

CHRIS: But if she is busy, I don't want to ... I mean –

NAY MIN: No, no. I want it, I want it. Come – Come – Maya! Let us sit. All sit.

Still cross, she sits.

NAY MIN: You have to understand, my dear, that Christopher Gunness is a hero to anybody old enough to remember the 1988 Revolution.

MAYA: I know. I was at the Reception. *(Turns to CHRIS – sharp.)* Were you followed?

Both CHRIS and NAY MIN taken aback by her tone.

CHRIS: I am sorry?

MAYA: Were you followed? Did you look to see if you were being followed?

CHRIS: I...

NAY MIN: *(Pacifying.)* So, so, so...

CHRIS: I didn't think. ... I was told that now it is different –

MAYA: Not true. Ko Tin Nyo's uncle met one of the recently released political prisoners – just MET him, in the street, by chance, no more– and he was arrested, put into Insein Gaol. Maybe they will arrest Uncle for meeting you!

CHRIS: I had no idea...I am so sorry! The message said to –

NAY MIN: No, no. She is right. But I decided I wanted to see you. We are here – let us talk. I don't think they will send me to prison again! I will make too much trouble. What if I die there this time? *(Laughs.)* Please – Mister Christopher, tell my young cousin why you call me Eastern Star and how you became a Burmese hero. I want this to be known.

CHRIS: But if Maya doesn't... does this interest you?

MAYA: Yes... *(Then.) Yes.*

NAY MIN: She knows nothing! I told you – she is smart, she is my dear cousin, my housekeeper, my everything, but she knows nothing. Twenty-five years old, born at the same time as the Revolution she grew up in a prison – not like me in a real prison, in Insein Jail but a prison – secrecy, fear, no proper newspapers, no proper school – she was lucky her parents had a little money to pay for a tutor, she studied accountancy, much cleverer than me, but still she knows nothing, this beautiful country she grew up in nothing but a prison, a desert –

MAYA: Uncle it wasn't exactly like that –

NAY MIN: And now all she wants, all so many of them want is money, car, house, whatnot. We must tell her, we must show her Mister Christopher, we must show her what we fought for, why we fought! You were a hero to so many of us in Burma. Talk to her!

CHRIS: Not me, Eastern Star, you were the hero. And ... whatever it was that I became here – not a hero, not at all – it was by complete accident. I was just a kid. A rookie.

MAYA: Rookie?

CHRIS: Novice. With the BBC. That's the –

MAYA: I know BBC.

CHRIS: I was a reporter for the World Service.

NAY MIN: Reporter for BBC World Service. See? Very important. Tell, tell!

CHRIS: Well ... I wasn't long out of University. Only been with the BBC a short while. My editor, my boss, got wind that something big was happening in Myanmar, in Burma and sent me out here. The BBC wasn't popular then – don't suppose the Generals like us now – and I had to go undercover. Tourist visa. Backpacker. All very cloak-and-dagger. I stayed at the Strand

MAYA: Back packer at the Strand?

NAY MIN: In those days, very poor hotel, not like now, 5 Star, Presidential Suite and whatnot. Listen, listen!

CHRIS: So ... there I was pretending to be a back packer, nosing around, sniffing the breezes and not getting anything very solid. Until one evening I came back to the hotel –

NAY MIN: This is good, very good – listen!

CHRIS: I went up to my room and found a handwritten note under my pillow –

NAY MIN: From me!

CHRIS: From you?

NAY MIN: Yes, yes, yes! I said what to write. Daughter of my client – I defended him in court, a Muslim he –

MAYA: A Muslim?

NAY MIN: Of course. Muslims need lawyers. Why not?

MAYA: No ... no ... I am sorry. Yes.

NAY MIN: So, so ... my client's daughter she worked there on telephones. She heard this hotshot BBC man talking to London in very loud voice, loud, loud – reporter, you know? – and all around military and intelligence and whatnot!

CHRIS: Oh my God, I had no idea!

NAY MIN: She called me. I arranged it. I told her to put note under the pillow! Me! You see?

CHRIS: *(Laughing, embarrassed.)* Oh God…I told you – rookie!… Anyway – the note said – Go to the Sulei Pagoda at 8.00 tomorrow and you will learn something of importance. Well, that doesn't happen every day so, of course, I did.

MAYA has her head down, still apparently sulking.

NAY MIN: Sulei Pagoda – listen, listen!

MAYA: I am listening, Uncle.

NAY MIN: This story is for you! For all you young people. But also my story. You say you do not know. Nobody knows. Now you will hear – my story. This man will tell. *(To CHRIS.)* Go, go!

CHRIS: Well…I hung around for a bit pretending to be a tourist. Then a young man approached me – young and furtive then, now the well rounded U Ba Swe, Chair of the Jubilee Reunion Committee, you probably met him *(MAYA nods.)* – he offered to be my guide. As I was explaining that I didn't want a guide, he whispered to me to follow him – but to keep my distance. He took me down side streets to what looked like an empty building. In one of the derelict rooms there were a few more young men like him, smoking a great deal, talking quietly, keeping watch out of windows. Is this what you want me to tell her?

NAY MIN: Yes, yes! Continue – please, please! All of it! She must hear. I have waited many years. My plan. Now you are here – Maya, my family must hear. Go, go!

Beat.

CHRIS: Right. So … I had my small portable recorder and
they gave me a cracking good interview about the horrors
of the military junta –

NAY MIN: Police State! Police State! Dictatorship. The richest
country in Asia made bankrupt. One night the *kyat*
destroyed. "Demonetised". Overnight. Notes destroyed.
Phhhft! Like that. Generals all at once very rich,
everybody else at once poor. Overnight. All savings gone.
Burma bankrupt. The Generals stole our money. *Phhhft!*
Go on, Mister Christopher, go on!

CHRIS: Well … the students told me they were going to
overthrow the government, kick the army out. To a young
reporter all gold dust. I knew that students in Burma
had a long tradition of political activism – going back to
Colonial days – so I thought this was par for the course.
What I hadn't noticed – or hadn't paid much attention
to – was that a couple of sentences had been in Burmese,
which of course I didn't understand. Clever.

NAY MIN: Clever? I told them! That was what I told them to do.

CHRIS: Really?

NAY MIN: Of course! Of course!

CHRIS: Oh … OK.

NAY MIN: Certainly. Planned by me. All planned.

CHRIS: Well – all I knew was that the interview tape had to
get to the BBC as soon as possible so I approached the
British Ambassador –

NAY MIN: Good man. Morland. Supporter. I knew him.

CHRIS: I asked him if he could send the tape by diplomatic
bag. Quite illegal, of course, but he agreed. Yes – a good
man. And so it got to the BBC. Luckily the editor that

night was a sympathiser or the interview might never have gone out.

MAYA: Why?

CHRIS: They were just students. Kids. Why should anybody take what they were saying seriously?

MAYA: And why lucky? You said –

CHRIS: Oh – because the sentence in Burmese said that on the 8th minute of the 8th hour of the 8th day of the 8th month of that year, 1988, the Burmese students would rise against the military junta and overthrow them in the name of the people. World Service went all over Burma. Everybody knew what was happening. What they could do. Should do.

NAY MIN: There! Did you know this? Did you?

MAYA: No, Uncle …

NAY MIN: You see? They don't know! All hidden. Their history all hidden!

CHRIS: Of course I had no idea what had been said. I didn't even know that eight was a lucky number for the Burmese.

NAY MIN: Lucky for the President. Lucky for the President! His luck, his stars – not ours!

CHRIS: Anyway, the broadcast went out on August the 6th and sure enough on August 8th at 8 minutes past 8 –

LX snap cross to CHRIS now back lit in tight spot in profile, face in shadow, mic in hand.

Distant sound of riots.

CHRIS: Hello BBC… Traffic please …Thank you… Chris Gunness from Rangoon, … OK. Thank you… Signal

37

begins … *(Reporter mode.)* This morning the 8th of August at exactly 8 minutes past 8 o'clock tens of thousands of Burmese people took to the streets of the capital Rangoon to demonstrate their dissatisfaction with the military junta that has ruled Burma for the last twenty-six years. They are demanding that the army steps aside and that multi-party elections are held. The Generals have so far made no response to the move but the atmosphere on the streets is tense. Western diplomats are warning that there could be bloodshed if the standoff continues. This is Christopher Gunness, BBC Rangoon.

Sound fades

LX resume general state.

MAYA: *(Now enthralled.)* Then what happened? How did you and Uncle meet?

NAY MIN: I went to see the Ambassador. I asked him to put me in touch with this Christopher Gunness.

CHRIS: The Ambassador called me in. Suggested that if I was going to work with this activist, human rights lawyer and general troublemaker U Nay Min it might be dangerous for him and that we ought to use a code name. He suggested Eastern Star. And lo! Our Eastern Star!

NAY MIN: We had found our voice.

CHRIS: And I my source. Quite by accident I found I had fired the starting gun on a revolution!

MAYA, now hooked, applauds.

CHRIS: We were a team, Eastern Star, weren't we?

NAY MIN: Oh yes … team.

Beat.

CHRIS: *(Picking up on NAY MIN's tone.)* So why …?

He flounders.

NAY MIN: Why … ?

CHRIS: *(Changing tack.)* Why did you pick me? There were other journalists you could have chosen.

NAY MIN: None as young and inexperienced as you!

He laughs heartily but the anger is there. CHRIS joins in less heartily.

CHRIS: I see… You were using me?

NAY MIN: You weren't using me?

Beat.

CHRIS: Fair enough. But it was good, wasn't it? We made a good team.

NAY MIN: Of course. You believed everything I told you didn't you?

CHRIS: *(Uncertain.)* I … Yes, I think so. Shouldn't I have done?

NAY MIN: Trees across the road? Road block?

CHRIS: I remember.

NAY MIN: Not true. *(Breaks out laughing.)* But the army – they believed! And so the students could travel freely. Wrong news but also good news! You see?

NAY MIN chuckling. CHRIS not.

CHRIS: Sort of.

NAY MIN: And others. Wrong news. Yes. Not big things. Just little things All for the revolution. You don't mind, Mister Christopher?

CHRIS: My job was telling the truth. I do mind a little.

NAY MIN: Unimportant. Yes – we were a team. The beginning of a journey. For both of us. This young rookie reporter went on to international fame and fortune, this old fool went on to prison, torture, and obscurity.

Pause. The tone has totally changed.

MAYA moves to him.

MAYA: Uncle...

NAY MIN: *(Brushing her off.)* Joke, joke, silly joke.

Beat. MAYA resumes her seat.

CHRIS: Is that the other reason you didn't want to see me? *(Silence from NAY MIN.)* Oh God ... Do you imagine I haven't thought of that? That's why I wanted so much to see you.

NAY MIN: To say sorry? Sorry that you were lucky and I was unlucky?

CHRIS: Oh ... more than that. We Brits carry guilt wherever we go, you must know that. Or we should. We insisted on a making a country out of so many different people. Not just the Burmese, the Shans, Karens, Kachins – to say nothing of the wretched Rohingya. We left a mess and you are still paying the price. Then I swan in here, stir things up, get great stories from you and skip back to safety.

NAY MIN: All long before you were born Mister Christopher. Not your fault. And if it was we Buddhists are taught to forgive. Of course I forgive. Not your fault. And yes we were a good team. *(To MAYA.)* We were part of something important. Important to you and your generation. Even though you know nothing about it.

MAYA: Why Uncle?

NAY MIN: Why do you know nothing about it? I told you – history was erased. They saw to that. The Generals did not want you to know.

MAYA: I understand that, but why is that time so important to us?

NAY MIN: So, so, so ... It was the beginning for The Lady. Daw Suu the daughter of our founder, Bogyoke Aung San, perhaps now nearly seventy years after his death to become our democratic leader. Important days, my dear. Our students opened the door to power for her. Our journey back to democracy. It began then in 1988.

MAYA: Daw Suu was a student?

NAY MIN laughs.

NAY MIN: No not student! She was married to a Britisher – another Britisher, Britishers everywhere – a professor at Oxford University, and she was visiting her sick mother in Burma when our revolution began. That was how she entered the world political stage.

MAYA: Because of the Students' Revolution?

NAY MIN: Students' Revolution, Students' Revolution – NAY MIN'S Revolution! Nay Min's Revolution gave birth to Daw Aung San Suu Kyi. *(Beat – wry.)* My fault. All my fault.

Shocked silence.

MAYA: Your fault? Uncle, why didn't you tell me all this?

Beat.

NAY MIN: Perhaps I thought you wouldn't want to listen.

Pause. MAYA retreats.

CHRIS: *(Tactfully.)* It is true. You were the architect.

NAY MIN: Architect, architect... Who knows? The revolution
– the first of its kind, its secret – there were no leaders. Not
on the street. Just... anger...The generals did not know
who to arrest, who to ... *(Snaps fingers.)*

MAYA shudders.

CHRIS: *(Quietly.)* The revolution was the first of its kind in
many ways. The people against their dictators. After
Myanmar, Tianaman Square, Indonesia, later the Arab
Spring. Your Uncle ran it, he brought everybody out on
strike, a general strike, journalists throughout the country
turned to him, he controlled it all. He ran the revolution
with his ear attached to his telephone.

NAY MIN grins, impish again.

NAY MIN: I did! I did!

*LX snap cross to NAY MIN back lit in tight spot, face in darkness,
phone to his ear.*

Rumble of people demonstrating on the streets, chanting.

NAY MIN: *(Urgent, young.)* Chris, Chris, take this down ... Big
news, I have persuaded the dockers. Tomorrow they will
be coming out on the streets in support of the students.
And what is more –

LX snap cross to CHRIS as before back lit in profile with mic

CHRIS: The dockers' support for the student uprising is now
being followed by many members of the Tatmadaw, the
Burmese Army, Navy and Air Force taking to the streets
in support of the student demands, as a groundswell of
dissatisfaction and anger spreads throughout the city with
further reports of organized opposition throughout the
country. Diplomats say the key question is now – how will
the military government respond?

LX resume general state. Fade sound.

MAYA breathless.

NAY MIN: So, so, so you must understand, my dear, it was the only news that our people could trust. Chris Gunness on the BBC World Service. Our household name.

CHRIS: Chris Gunness was the puppet. You pulled the strings. I was not taking risks like you. Hell I wasn't even there after a while.

MAYA: You left the country?

CHRIS: I ... I didn't want to! My visa had run out. The Embassy told me I should leave as I had become what they politely termed " toxic", that I was going to create a diplomatic incident. *(Beat.)* Something else I have always been ashamed about.

NAY MIN: Something else? What else?

CHRIS: I meant ... *(Falters again.)* More guilt. Always guilt. The journalist's burden. Stupid, stupid. *(They stare at him puzzled.)* No ... just that ... deserting you ...

Pause.

NAY MIN: *(Kind.)* You had no choice ... And you remained our voice.

CHRIS: In Dahka.

NAY MIN: Still our voice.

Beat.

MAYA: *(Tactfully.)* Daw Suu ... You say she –

NAY MIN: Daw Suu ... Yes, yes. So, so ... Our Revolution helped her to grow – how do you say? – into her skin. Become a leader

MAYA: How?

NAY MIN: She found the meaning of her life. No longer an Oxford housewife but her father's daughter. Burma's saviour.

MAYA: You sound ... was that bad, Uncle?

NAY MIN: Politics has many colours. Not all rosy.

MAYA: I know that!

Beat.

NAY MIN: She has made friends with my enemies.

Pause.

CHRIS: She 'sought accommodation' with them, perhaps?

MAYA: Isn't it because of her that we can have this conversation today with Mister Gunness?

NAY MIN laughs, claps.

NAY MIN: Very good, my dear. You are right, you are right. She has taken us on a long journey. All praise to her for that. May she take us yet further. But remember where it began. It was the revolution that made her famous.

MAYA: How?

NAY MIN and CHRIS exchange a look.

NAY MIN: *(Back to MAYA, gleeful.)* She announced that she would lead a march of her supporters through the city. The Generals forbade it. She said she would ignore them. I went to a friend's house on the route where I knew the army would try to block her. I watched from the roof. I called Chris. In Dhaka.

Snap cross to NAY MIN in back lit tight spot, telephone to his ear.

NAY MIN: *(Tense, urgent.)* There must be forty, maybe fifty soldiers, Christopher, all armed, spread out across the road. No sign yet of the NLD march but I think any minute now...

Add in tight spot on CHRIS back lit in profile mic in hand.

CHRIS: As Daw Aung San Suu Kyi approached the military road block leading her long column of National League for Democracy supporters – estimated at well over a thousand – there was no move from the soldiers until she was within hailing distance...

We hear a distant male voice callling "halt!"

NAY MIN: The officer at the head of the roadblock has given a command and the soldiers behind him have immediately dropped to a kneeling position, guns at their shoulders pointing at the demonstrators. If she ignores them this could be a bloodbath, the end of everything ... This is awful, Christopher, this is so bad ...

CHRIS: On receiving the command to halt and proceed no further, the column of demonstrators faltered and came to a halt. Onlookers were terrified there was going to be a bloodbath. Daw Aung San Suu Kyi stepped forward...

We hear the distant voice of Daw Aung San Suu Kyi as though coming through the phone speaking just before NAY MIN passes it on to CHRIS.

NAY MIN: "I demand the right to make my peaceful protest" she is saying ... " I am asking my followers to stay where they are while I alone march forward. If any of the young men ... from our beloved Tatmadaw that my father founded at the birth of our Independence ...... wish to shoot his daughter they must answer to their own consciences ..." I cannot believe what I am seeing, Christopher, I cannot believe it ...

CHRIS: As this lone woman stepped forward the officer in charge repeatedly called on her to stop. She ignored him and continued to march steadily forward until –

NAY MIN: *(Screaming with excitement.)* The soldiers have put up their weapons ... They are breaking up ... Moving to the side of the road ... She is walking between them ...

Sound of applause and cheering.

CHRIS: Behind her the astonished column of her followers now marched after her cheering and clapping the soldiers who had made way for them. Onlookers said they felt they had witnessed a miracle ...

Sound fades. Lights resume.

A silence as all three contemplate the enormity of the event.

NAY MIN: Her door.

CHRIS: And the door to Burma's democracy.

MAYA: So she had won?

NAY MIN: Some said so.

MAYA: What do you mean Uncle?

NAY MIN: What is winning? Has she won Mister Christopher? Will she win?

CHRIS: What do you think?

NAY MIN: I think we don't know. I think we must wait and see.

CHRIS: ... Eastern Star what are you saying?

NAY MIN: I am saying that on that day yes – she won. But will she win? Outside is easy. But inside? To govern? So many problems. What you say – the Shans, the Kachins, the Karens, the Rohingyas. People say we are gentle. But are

46

we? Our army? Gentle? We are Buddhists, we are tolerant aren't we? Towards Muslims? Rohingyas? The truth, the sad truth, we are not yet a nation. So how to govern us? We must wait and see – no?

And that is clearly all they are going to get.

CHRIS: Yes. The story went everywhere. Biblical. The parting of the Red Sea.

MAYA: Uncle I didn't know you were ... at the centre.

CHRIS: The architect. The quiet architect.

NAY MIN: One of them. There were others.

MAYA: But so important! I knew you were a hero, a political prisoner but ... my mother never told me.

NAY MIN: She didn't know. Many people disappeared, went underground. And I was – how do you call, the black sheep. I didn't want her to be in danger.

MAYA: Why don't we all know about it?

NAY MIN: I told you! You haven't been allowed to! It has all been buried. And you learned, so many of you learned not to look at the past, only the future. And now even my tired old head is forgetting... But yes, Myanmar is changing and this man, the voice of the Revolution who told our story not only to us but to the world ... he has brought it all back. And you are hearing my story. Someone is hearing my story. *(To CHRIS.)* Thank you.

He is getting tearful.

MAYA: Is that hard Uncle?

NAY MIN: A little, perhaps.

MAYA: Why? Because you didn't win?

NAY MIN: For many reasons, but for that, yes.

MAYA: So why didn't you win?

Beat.

NAY MIN: I made a mistake.

CHRIS: You did?

NAY MIN: Oh yes. Nay Min did good things. Chris Gunness did good things. But this was a mistake. And Chris Gunness made it worse.

CHRIS: Did I?

NAY MIN: You remember the army officer?

CHRIS: Not sure...

NAY MIN: The one who told the truth about the Tatmadaw.

CHRIS: Oh God, yes.

NAY MIN: *(To MAYA.)* He told how the army, the beloved Tatmadaw were torturing prisoners, all that, using children to walk ahead of them as they advanced so the children would be blown up by any mines that had been set, little children being killed to make a safe path for the soldiers. We all knew – we *knew*! That was why it was so bad – we knew it was happening but here an honest man, a soldier, was prepared to say so. I gave the story to Chris.

MAYA: Did you broadcast it?

CHRIS: I had no reason to doubt it. And, yes, suddenly the world sat up. There were speeches in the UN, in Congress, the House of Commons, broadcasts, newspaper articles all over the world bitterly attacking the generals. It was amazing, but apparently ... ?

NAY MIN: Yes. It was not good.

MAYA: Why not?

NAY MIN: Daw Suu and President Ne Win had known each other for years. The Generals were not frightened by her, not then. But this was different. The whole world was attacking them. They had become, what do you call, pariahs. They did not like that.

MAYA: So?

NAY MIN: They acted.

Snap cross to CHRIS in tight back lit spot with mic

Sound of miltary boots running, whistles, gun shots.

CHRIS: Reports are coming in of mass military deployment in Rangoon and throughout the country as the Army rounds up rebel students and other dissidents imprisoning and massacring them apparently at random. No figures can be confirmed but deaths are estimated by diplomats to run to many hundreds. In one case some forty young men were locked in the back of a Black Maria in temperatures of 40 degrees and left in there overnight without food or water. The following morning their bodies were found heaped on top of each other. Every single one had suffocated.

Sound fades. Lights resume

Silence.

NAY MIN: So, so ... You see? We did not win. Parents still do not know what happened to their children. No bodies to bury. Do you hear me? You hear what I am saying? The soldiers burned the corpses of the students they killed so nobody would know. The sky above the city was black with smoke. I wanted to die. Listen ... The student's music. The students singing the revolution's what-do-you-call ... anthem.

He presses the control on his walkman. He lets it play a moment then switches it off.

NAY MIN: Beautiful, no?

Silence.

MAYA: Oh Uncle ... that is so awful, so sad! But now – because of what you did then – we are winning now?

NAY MIN: We do not know yet, child. I hope you will be free. Free to build your chain of hotels. But we don't yet know. *(Turns to CHRIS.)* You look ... What is the matter?

CHRIS: Is that what you believe?

NAY MIN: Is what what I believe?

CHRIS: Do you really think that my broadcast about the army officer and the Tatmadaw atrocities were what led to the Junta turning so brutal?

NAY MIN: There were other reasons but – yes.

CHRIS: Oh God...

NAY MIN: I gave you the story Mister Christopher.

CHRIS: But my broadcast.

MAYA: You didn't kill. Either of you.

CHRIS: Still ...

NAY MIN: We – you – have more than blood on out hands, Mister Christopher.

CHRIS: Why?

NAY MIN: Our Revolution – and that broadcast – led to... *(To MAYA – impish again.)* Have you heard of the "We Don't Like the Look of You law"?

50

MAYA: No. What does it mean?

NAY MIN: HA! It meant that they could arrest anybody.
Throw them in jail. If they didn't like the look of them.
What we called it. If you made a joke about the generals
– prison. Go on the streets to protest, they shot you
dead. Universities closed down. Rangoon University
was famous, very good. Mandalay – closed. All closed.
Daw Suu put under house arrest for fifteen years. Many
thousands in prison. Including me. For sixteen years.

MAYA: You were in prison for sixteen years Uncle?

NAY MIN: I was.

MAYA: My mother told me you had been in prison but I
thought maybe six months, a year. Sixteen! How did you
survive?

NAY MIN: Survive? Ah, now, did I? Part of me perhaps. For
years I felt nothing. But slowly something, yes something
came back to life.

MAYA: But while you were in there? How?

NAY MIN: *(Shrugs.)* By learning to.

MAYA: What was it like?

NAY MIN: Breaking stones all day in the sun, ankles chained
together. Five, six, seven, more men in one cell. A dog's
kennel. With a hole in the floor.

MAYA: Ugh…

NAY MIN: Yes, not nice. Little food, often bad, little water.
Dysentery, scabies. Our constant companions *(Chuckles.)*
Oh, until that Swedish journalist at a Press conference
asked how my health was. The Minister apparently said
my health was excellent. The next day – the next day! – I
started getting fruit, vegetables – even meat. Would you

51

believe it? I never understood why. Not till many years later!

MAYA: All those men in so small a space. How did you sleep? Bunks? Did they give you bunks?

NAY MIN: The floor. *(Smiles.)* A tin plate for my pillow.

MAYA: Oh Uncle ...

NAY MIN: Don't be distressed. You have listened. Thank you.

MAYA overwhelmed.

CHRIS: Sixteen years? Did everyone who took part in the Revolution get sixteen years?

NAY MIN: Not all. Some fewer, some seven, some eight. Mostly eight. I got eight. Then when I came out I was rearrested and sent back for eight more.

CHRIS: Why?

Pause.

NAY MIN: For trying to contact you. Even though I never reached you. *(Beat.)* You never called back.

Pause.

CHRIS: Oh God ...

NAY MIN: Yes ...

MAYA: That is ... *(Angry.)* Why? Why did you not call back? Did you not get the message?

CHRIS: I ...

He shakes his head in despair.

CHRIS: No wonder ... No wonder you did not want to see me.

NAY MIN: Yes I was angry Mister Christopher. Very angry. About many things. Every day I still fight with my anger. I fight it and I hate it. My country was abandoned by the world. *(At CHRIS.)* *I* was abandoned,

CHRIS: ... I don't know what to –

NAY MIN: Nothing. You need say nothing. We have spoken. That is good. And I am tired now. Please... *(Gestures to CHRIS to leave.)*

Pause.

CHRIS stands. He hesitates by NAY MIN as though wanting to embrace him. NAY MIN shifts, signalling refusal. MAYA leads CHRIS out. We hear door open and shut. She comes back. NAY MIN's eyes are closed.

NAY MIN: He's gone?

MAYA: Gone.

NAY MIN: And you? Your swain will be waiting.

MAYA: I expect he's gone too.

NAY MIN: Ah. I am sorry.

Pause.

MAYA: Thank you, Uncle.

NAY MIN: For what?

MAYA: Making me stay.

NAY MIN: You learned?

MAYA: Yes.

NAY MIN: And that was good?

MAYA: Yes. And for you?

NAY MIN: Me?

MAYA: He is your friend again? I think ..

NAY MIN: What?

MAYA: He wants to be.

NAY MIN: Well ... Perhaps. We shall see. So ... now you can have your day off.

MAYA: Go to sleep.

NAY MIN remains still.

NAY MIN: I told you. Like a baby.

He sleeps.

MAYA watches.

Lights refocus. Spot up on JAKE in London on phone.

JAKE: Did you know?

Spot up on CHRIS on phone in hotel.

CHRIS: What?

MAYA kisses the sleeping NAY MIN on forehead and exits. Lights down on Yangon apartment.

JAKE: That was why he was rearrested?

CHRIS: No idea ... I couldn't speak, Jake, couldn't say anything. There was ... It was too awful ...

JAKE: Jesus, Chris, you mustn't beat yourself up over this!

CHRIS: Jake, he went to prison because he tried to contact me. Just trying to contact me was enough to get him eight years! And a call I never returned.

JAKE: That was because he was living under an evil, fucked
up regime, not just because –

CHRIS: He risked his life, I reported it all – from bloody
Bangladesh half the time Of course I beat myself up. I
have for twenty-five years! I failed him. Not just me, many
of us failed him. You don't know the half of it.

JAKE: Well?

Beat.

CHRIS: I knew he had tried to call me! All right? I bloody
well knew! And I did nothing. There! I went to the
Foreign Office, asked for advice. They said it would only
make things worse for him if I returned his call. "Honestly
– not a good idea, Chris. Really don't advise it." Smarmy
bastard. Calling me Chris like we were old friends. Baby
faced high bloody flyer. "Destined for the top" written all
over him. Ugh … So what did I do? I did as I was told.
What the mandarins told me. What suited them. Suited
the bloody suits. And … yes, me. I didn't return a call
from a man who deserved … everything. What can I
say? And I should have persuaded the BBC to speak up
for him to accredit him as a stringer, that little letter with
BBC heading would have given him at least some kind of
status, protection.

JAKE: Wouldn't that have …

CHRIS: What?

JAKE: Put him at risk? More risk? Anyway he was your
source, he wasn't a stringer he was an activist. His choice.
A politician. He knew the risks. Is it the BBC's job to –

CHRIS: It was what he asked for! What the man on the
ground asked for. Surely he knew better than the Foreign
Office – or the bloody BBC! It would have been *something.*

55

He risked his life, this one extraordinary man taking on an army, orchestrating a revolution! We got – I got – many, many stories from him, the World Service at its best, shining a light in darkness, what it was supposed to do, and the BBC – that international symbol for freedom of speech and fair play – would not stand up for him. It betrayed him – as did I. I should have tried harder, should have made them do it!

Silence.

JAKE: Is that what the nightmares were about?

CHRIS: Probably.

JAKE: All the things you couldn't say to me?

Pause.

CHRIS: Some. Not all.

Lights refocus to Yangon apartment. JAKE exits. NAY MIN gathers two glasses of soft drink as CHRIS goes to him.

NAY MIN: Maya makes these much better. But I try. *(CHRIS takes glass.)* I wanted to see you alone before she gets here. I thought she had had enough of my old man's talk, history. I wanted her to meet you because I wanted her to learn. And it was good. She says so herself. I think maybe she now thinks politics, human rights are more important than money. *(Smiles.)* Well – as important. So – is good. A beginning. Thank you. But I wanted to see you alone.

CHRIS: You want to see me now Eastern Star. You didn't. You were angry. And I don't blame you.

Pause.

NAY MIN: Not very good Buddhism.

CHRIS: Aren't Buddhists allowed to be angry?

NAY MIN: It has been hard, Mister Christopher.

CHRIS: I am sure.

NAY MIN: Now, I think ... did it happen? Did any of it happen? The students, Ba Swe and the others they make out that I am just a vain old man, a forgotten part of the struggle. I am the forgotten man.

CHRIS: Not by me.

NAY MIN: You ... Yes, you. Yesterday ... That Maya should hear my story. Just one person in my family. And you were there to help me tell it. Thank you. Mister Christopher, can you understand this? It is my belief – my honest belief – that if Myanmar doesn't learn from what happened on 8.8.88 we will never move forward. Never!

CHRIS: Of course I understand.

NAY MIN: And my Maya was a start. My witness. She heard my story.

CHRIS: The story of Eastern Star.

NAY MIN: Yes. And others, many others. But yes.

CHRIS: So why didn't you want to see me? Because I had told the story that you had risked your life for? I took the glory and you took the pain?

NAY MIN: Yes. Yes, yes. You wrote my story. My history. All true. So, so ... *(Shrugs.)* Doesn't the writer always own history more than the one who makes it?

CHRIS: Not what I intended. You must know that. But ... You went to jail and I was free. And I didn't return your call. Because of me you were sent back into jail for another eight years. So many reasons you have to be angry with me. And me – eternally – with myself.

NAY MIN: Anger, yes. So much anger.

CHRIS: You are angry and yet you thank me. As your friend.

NAY MIN: Angry and not angry. Life always has two faces – do you not know that?

CHRIS: Will you write it now? Your story, the true story?

NAY MIN: Perhaps. If I am spared.

CHRIS: Spared? *(NAY MIN shrugs eloquently. Will not be drawn.)* Well … in that case you will own your history …

NAY MIN: There is more.

CHRIS: Ah.

NAY MIN: *Why* did you not return my call?

CHRIS: I … have no answer. No good answer. I am … ashamed. More ashamed than I can ever say.

NAY MIN: Sixteen years. That is a lot of anger.

CHRIS: I understand.

NAY MIN: No. You don't. Look –

NAY MIN suddenly stands and loosens his aingyi. He lifts the back up and turns away from CHRIS to show him the scars. CHRIS flinches.

NAY MIN: This Maya has never seen. She must not see…

CHRIS: What… What is it?

NAY MIN: Whips. And if they really wanted to punish us we were made to crawl over rocks on our bellies. Jagged rocks. Like razors.

He turns round opening the front of his aingyi. His chest a mass of scars. CHRIS recoils.

CHRIS: Jesus …

NAY MIN: The whipping wasn't the worst. The electric shock treatment. *(As he buttons the aingyi back he mock theatrically demonstrates the spasm, screams – then grins.)* ... Weights dropped on the belly... Tied up and bound like a ball, a *chinlon* ball for hours, days, no food, no water ... And sometimes I thought of you ... *(Anger taking over again.)* This is hard, so hard! ... I wondered what you were doing, where you were..

CHRIS: I am so sorry ... So sorry ...

NAY MIN: You did not know? *(CHRIS shakes his head.)* You did not *guess? (CHRIS speechless.)* You knew about torture? *(Chris nods.)* So how could you not guess – maybe you did not know – but how could you not guess about me?

CHRIS: I ...

NAY MIN: You did not want to know.

CHRIS: Probably.

Pause.

NAY MIN: Well ... Yes. I understand that. Hard. But I understand. Yes.

CHRIS: I am sorry.

NAY MIN stares unforgivingly at CHRIS' bowed head for a disconcerting length of time.

NAY MIN: That was another reason I changed my mind about meeting you.

CHRIS: Yes?

NAY MIN: I wanted you to know.

CHRIS: What?

NAY MIN: THIS! I wanted you to know my anger.

CHRIS: I don't know what... I don't know what to say...

Pause.

NAY MIN: There is more.

CHRIS: Oh God...

NAY MIN: How did it begin? Have you thought of that? *(The anger suppurating now, his fists clenched.)* Please understand me, I am trying so hard here, so hard ... I must not hate, I must not hate ...

CHRIS: What now? ... What are you saying?

NAY MIN: The beginning. Just after they destroyed our revolution. Why did they arrest me? I had been so careful, so secret. How did they find me? Someone betrayed me. Someone who had my number gave it to Military Intelligence. You had my number. I don't want to believe this – but was it you?

Silence. CHRIS is cracking. He slumps to his knees, weeping.

CHRIS: ... I can't ... I can't ... do this ... I can't bear you to think ...

He sobs.

NAY MIN watches him.

After a while he gets down beside CHRIS and puts his arm round his shoulders.

NAY MIN: No ... no ... We were a team. I ... No. I didn't want to believe it. Maya is right. Friends. Understand me, all those years in prison, so lonely, the mind goes on strange journeys. No, not you, it wasn't you. I am sure now it wasn't you. Friends. Always friends. Sh ... Sh ...We were a team. A good team. We made a little bit of history together ... Good history ... Sh ... Sh...

CHRIS is still sobbing.

Lights refocus to London as JAKE enters.

JAKE: *(To CHRIS on the floor.)* No more nightmares?

CHRIS gathers himself slowly and goes across to JAKE.

CHRIS: Can't promise that.

NAY MIN watches him go then returns thoughtfully to his writing.

JAKE: Drink?

CHRIS: Please.

JAKE pours CHRIS a glass of wine, takes it to him.

JAKE: So how have you left it?

CHRIS: Sort of ... OK, I think.

JAKE waits.

CHRIS: Not really OK.

JAKE: Why?

CHRIS takes a drink.

CHRIS: It's hard to... *(Another sip. Silence.)*

JAKE: Try.

Pause.

CHRIS: I didn't ... In the end I couldn't even tell him...

JAKE: What?

CHRIS: Twenty-five years... Haven't told anybody...

JAKE: *Try.*

Pause.

CHRIS: It is possible... I ... don't know ... It might have been ... It might have been me ... Might have been me who betrayed him ... I hope it wasn't, God how I hope it wasn't but I did give his number to someone ... Someone I trusted ... Someone in London ... They might have passed it on...

JAKE: That doesn't mean. –

CHRIS: Two hours later ... Two hours after I passed on the number the news came through that Nay Min had been arrested.

Pause.

JAKE: That still doesn't mean ...

CHRIS: I know, I know, I know it doesn't! BUT – but, but, but ...

JAKE: Chris ...

CHRIS: Yes, of course there is no way of knowing for certain! But how do you live with that? All these years, I have been ... tortured by thought that I might have betrayed him, I didn't mean to, God knows, I didn't, he was a hero, my hero, it has been unbearable, that's why I wanted to see him, wanted so much to see him and when it came to it I didn't have the courage to tell him. Tell him that it might have been me that betrayed him.

JAKE: But you don't know that it was you Chris. You don't know ...

CHRIS: Listen to what I am saying Jake! *Listen* to me!

JAKE: You loved him. That is the reality, isn't it? He wasn't just a political activist doing his job – as you were doing yours. You grew to love him.

Pause.

62

CHRIS: That's ... probably the truth ... I think I did. Not lovers , never lovers. But love, yes, I think I did. He didn't know it, of course. This passionate human rights lawyer. This passionate father figure. You know my weakness for older men. *(JAKE smiles.)* That's probably why... all this ...

Pause.

JAKE: I wish you had been able to tell me.

CHRIS: *(Nods.)* I am sorry. I buried it. Until that email came in. Didn't tell anyone. He told me his story and I didn't tell him mine, the story I was too ashamed to admit to anyone – even you! – my fear, my utter gut-twisting horror that has been eating me for twenty-five years that I might have betrayed a man I loved ... Oh Jake – what can I do?

Pause.

JAKE: I guess you have made a start. You *have* told me.

CHRIS: Yes.

CHRIS reaches out to put his hand on JAKE's arm in gratitude.

Lights refocus on NAY MIN still writing.

Build sound of students singing their 88 protest 'anthem' of defiance and hope.

MAYA enters, puts a cup of tea beside NAY MIN. He acknowledges it with a nod. She goes to sit, reading the Mynamar times as he continues to write his story and the anthem builds.

Slow fade to black.

END

WWW.OBERONBOOKS.COM

Follow us on Twitter @oberonbooks
& Facebook @OberonBooksLondon